# *MY SECRET*

*The true story of one woman's adoption discovery and search*

*Joanne E. Sayre*

# FORWARD

I received encouragement from many people; friends, family, and professional social workers, to write down the experiences of my search for my birth mother. For me, there was an obvious difficulty. I am a person that likes to get to the point without all of the fine minutia. However, in order to do justice to my journey I needed to reveal the sometimes unattractive workings of my life for all to see.

My hope is that the reader will be encouraged in their own journey; their own search for truth.

My odyssey lasted forty years with dead ends at every turn. I often found myself discouraged, but never gave up. The truth was that important to me.

*Soli Deo Gloria*

## INTRODUCTION

*According to the North American Adoption Congress in New York City, more than 60,000 people are currently involved in the search process. Birth mothers are seeking children they gave up for adoption, and children are hunting for birth parents. The search effort has grown in intensity in the last twenty years from an individual effort to a national movement (Cronin 90.) The search is made more difficult because adoption records are sealed by the courts. However, the rising sentiment in our society concerning adoptee rights provides stirring argument for removing the "seal of secrecy."*

This was the opening paragraph for a research paper I wrote over twenty years ago for a college English course. My paper was entitled, "Adoption — The Seal of Secrecy."

In 1971 adoption rights came to the forefront by a champion for the cause, Florence Fisher, founder of the Adoptees Liberty Movement Association (ALMA.) She successfully found her birth mother after a twenty-year search.

*Introduction*

This was just the first of many organizations to follow "through court challenges, reform of state legislation, and initiatives to pursue their agenda to repeal laws that sealed adoption records." (Encyclopedia of Children and Childhood in History and Society) There was even an offshoot internet-based adoption activist organization, Bastard Nation.

During the many years of my search, several organizations came to be such as Official Birth Registry, My Heritage.com, Adoption Search and Reunion Support Group, Adult Adoption Support Group, Social Services for Searching Adults, and Adoptees in Search, to name a few.

According to Adoption USA, a national association of adoptive parents, a 2007 survey found that 99% of adopted children ages five and under know that they are adopted. My how times have changed.

I was born in 1952. A child born to an unwed mother during this time would carry the stigma of being illegitimate. No need to mention the situation or circumstance. The child was a bastard, less than. A young woman finding herself unwed, alone, and pregnant during the 50's had little or no choice but to give her child up for adoption.

3

There were no social services in place to help her keep and support her baby; no WIC, welfare, daycare, or affordable housing. Everything was kept a secret. Discretion was necessary to save the family from disgrace in the community.

When I first contacted The Maryland Department of Social Services, my social worker strongly suggested I read a book entitled, "The Girls Who Went Away" by Ann Fessler. I believe my social worker wanted me to have a better understanding concerning the culture of that time period and what my birth mother went through. This book captures the lives and thoughts of young woman who relinquished their legal rights to their newborn babies. Their stories are heartbreaking.

A statement from one of the birth mothers was, "I felt like I had no voice in the decision to give up my daughter. " Another woman was told that it "was in her best interest." Many women had been told they were trash, loose, worth nothing, and a total disappointment to their families.

After giving birth in the facility a young woman was told to go home, forget about it, put "it" behind them, and go on with their life and never speak of the experience.

The heart does not come with an off switch.

*In the beginning.....*

*"I don't have to be nice to you 'cause you're really not my cousin anyways. You're ADOPTED!"*

## CHAPTER ONE

*In the beginning.....*

Sometimes in your life there arrives a defining moment; one event that changes everything you were confident in. For me, that moment came when I was only seven years old and found out that I was ADOPTED.

My aunt had sent my ten-year-old male cousin outside to play and supervise his siblings; a five-year-old sister and two-year-old twins, a boy and a girl. I am very confident that he would have much rather been playing with the boys in the neighborhood, working on their tree fort in the woods or just creating some general mischief. I am also equally confident that he was given instructions to "play nice."

In the fifties, for the first eight years of my life, we lived next door to my aunt and uncle and their seven children. Our homes were only about two hundred feet apart. This was rather convenient for me as an only child to always have someone available to play with.

My aunt and uncle had a circle shaped driveway paved with loose stone. We used to pretend the grassy area inside the circle was an island and the stone covered driveway was the water surrounding it. Outside of the driveway, on the front lawns of both homes, we turned lawn chairs upside down to create forts. Blankets were borrowed from our houses and draped over the chairs to give an "authentic fort look." Old cardboard boxes became boats on "Stone River." We could play pirates, cowboys and Indians; anything we wanted. All that we needed was an active imagination. It was magical.

However, on this particular day, as I joined in the playtime on "our island," it was obviously the last straw for my cousin, more than he could deal with. He was already stuck watching and "being nice" to his siblings, let alone a cousin. Overwhelmed with his situation, it didn't take long before he vented his frustration and exploded at me.

"I don't have to be nice to you 'cause you're really not my cousin anyways. You're ADOPTED!" he hollered.

What? I couldn't breathe. I'm not your cousin? What does

6

# In the beginning.....

adopted mean? I just started running towards home. I couldn't
make sense of the words; but his delivery cut at my heart.

I burst into the house, tears streaming down my face, calling for my mother. When I relayed to her what had happened,
trying to find space for words between my sobs I expected to
be comforted and reassured that my cousin was wrong and just
being hurtful. Instead, my mother exploded into a tirade of anger
focused on her sister.

"Elsie had no right to tell anyone you are adopted. How dare
she open her mouth," Mother exploded. "She's going to pay for
this," she growled, her dark eyes flashing with anger.

I felt lost and alone and left without an explanation. Asking
again would only bring more anger from my mother.

There was no way to know that our afternoon playtime would
be the catalyst for a family war. Out the side door went my mother and straight over to my Aunt Elsie's house to confront her. My
mother and her sister engaged in verbal battle over my revelation.
There was screaming and shouting.

"You should have told her Hilda. You should have told the
child that you really were not her mother and she had been adopted," Aunt Elsie said.

7

The entire neighborhood could have heard it all, especially the volume of their exchange.

I stood on the porch, covering my ears to shield out the shouting.

"How dare you," my mother screamed. "You will pay for this!"

Chills ran over me. I had started a war. My heart beat so fast I could hardly breathe. I couldn't hear Aunt Elsie's reply.

"This is all your fault Elsie! You had no right to tell anyone she was adopted," Mother screamed.

The battle overshadowed everything in life, so big that I was ordered by my mother to not walk on my aunt and uncle's property. That meant that since my grandmother lived on the other side of their property I had to walk out our driveway and down the road to get to her house, and I loved going to my grandmom's house. It was a place of solace.

Grandmom was born in Germany in 1893 and immigrated to the United States as a seven-year indentured servant when she was twenty.

Grandmom was a very loving woman, but was not to be trifled with. She kept a switch behind her kitchen door in case one of

8

her grandchildren felt particularly "frisky." I was grateful to never experience the switch.

I can only recall being scolded by her on one occasion. I was in her living room when the news came on and the topic was policies of the Soviet Union and how they affect the free world. I blurted out, "I hate those Russians." She turned to face me and said, "Joanne, don't ever say that! Never hate a people because of their government. My brothers were members of the Nazi army. They had no choice. Nazi's came to our home and held a gun to my sister's head. If they did not join, the Nazi's said they would shoot her. My brother's did not want to go but they protected their sister. My brothers died in the war."

Wow, how does one respond to that? I promised her I would never say anything like that again.

She kept herself well groomed, with beautiful snow-white hair, short and softly curled, and a front buttoned housedress with the hem falling well below her knees. I remember watching her put on black low-heeled buttonhole shoes; the kind that required a special hook apparatus to close the buttons. And of course, always a clean pressed apron to complete her daily ensemble.

She never spoke German to her grandchildren. I suppose in

the late 50's and 60's the taste of WWII was still bitter and she wanted us to just "be Americans." But when she sat in her rocking chair crocheting during televised Baltimore Oriole's games, this passionate fan of the O's would verbalize her displeasure with Earl Weaver's calls in German.

Grandmom was an amazing cook who loved to feed her grandchildren. We were raised on homemade potato dumplings, noodles, bread — the list is endless. Nothing says love in a German home like the smell of yeast dough rising.

Soon after my revelation, I realized that everything I ever thought or knew about my family was wrong. I guess she really wasn't my grandmom. I didn't know what to think and because no one ever talked to me about it, I was led to the shocking realization that I was alone, different, and not a part of the family. I felt embarrassed. Now I understood what adopted meant.

## CHAPTER 2

*The big move......*

When I was nine we moved about twenty-five minutes away from my cousins and grandparents. I couldn't understand why we were moving. There was no warning.

My mother had only one cousin on her father's side and he had invited our little family of three to move in with him. Our family called him Uncle Gilbert. He was a wealthy confirmed bachelor. His home was located on Greenspring Avenue, a half mile from "the Valley." This area was best known for horse racing and horse breeding farms. The most well know was Sagamore Farms. All I saw was miles and miles of white fences and white barns with red roofs.

His home was large and he did not want to live alone. Although he was only in his early forties, he walked with a cane. The bones in his hips were deteriorating. Because of his condition and the intensity of the pain, he had cocktails everyday beginning at 4:30 p.m. Dinner was then scheduled at 5:30 p.m. daily.

This move was quite a change for me. I missed having my grandmom close and cousins and friends in the neighborhood to play with. It was so quiet in this house. There had never been a child living there before. I wasn't feeling very comfortable. "No running in the house Joanne," my mother would say. "Don't touch that. It might break, Joanne. Why don't you go outside and play?"

Play? Seriously? There was no one to play with except my dog.

How are you supposed to play "kick-the-can" by yourself? There was no one playing "it," no captives to free, only me. Catching lightning bugs was just not as much fun when doing it alone. We used to "borrow" a clear canning jar and poke holes in the lid so the bugs could breathe. This was our high-tech lantern.

Two more months and the leaves would begin to turn colors and then fall from the trees. There were many large oak and maple trees where I used to live. My older cousins would rake the leaves in patterns to form a leaf maze so we could all play Catchers on the Path. I was homesick already.

Since my mother's cousin didn't like cats, my parents had to give my cat away. I remember holding Freckles outside in the shed for the last time and crying in her fur as I held her to my face. He wanted my dog Rascal gone too, but Daddy put his foot down at that and Rascal stayed.

I felt very isolated; trapped. We had always lived in the country but this was even further out in the boonies. We needed to drive at least thirty minutes to get to the nearest store. And since my school, my church, and the grocery store were all within a few blocks of each other; it was thirty minutes to get anywhere of importance in my world.

My mother reminded me that the reason we moved was so that I could have more "advantages in life." At that time, I couldn't see any advantages in uprooting our family.

Not long after we moved into my Uncle's home, a construction crew arrived and began digging a massive hole in our front yard. Evidently, my Uncle had decided to build a bomb shelter in our front yard. The year was 1962.

John F. Kennedy had only been President for a year when the United States discovered Soviet missiles located in Cuba. The Soviets denied our country's accusation, but the United States had photos to prove the missiles' existence. This situation could have escalated into nuclear war, but ended a week later. The Soviet leader**,** Kruschev agreed to remove the missiles if Kennedy agreed to stay out of Cuba.

The bomb shelter was creepy. Its entrance was through a wall in the basement. In case of a nuclear attack all four of us would need to live, sleep, and eat in an eleven by fourteen foot room. I doubt we would have lasted a week. Eventually, it was used as a very expensive cold cellar to store canned goods.

# CHAPTER 3

*The purple beast.......*

Back in the day, we attended junior high school after elementary and the grades were seventh and eighth only. I had heard all the horror stories relating to junior high; spit balls in the hair, being picked up and sat on the water fountain while another bully turned it on. Let's add to that having to take group showers with twenty other girls after gym class, acne, combination locks on your hall and gym locker with number sequences that could easily be forgotten, and a much larger two story, three building facility to navigate.

The absolute worst was that I had grown three inches over the summer and was now the tallest person in my class. I was five foot eight inches tall, lanky, with black hair in a world dominated by blondes. My mother would not allow me to shave my legs so to cover the dark leg hair I wore a lot of knee-highs. All hopes of blending into the background were shattered.

For my first day of junior high and as an extra special gift, my

15

mother picked out a dress as a present from her and Dad. As I opened the box, my eyes could hardly believe the "treasure" hidden inside. It was probably the most grotesque frock ever designed. The entire dress took ugly to a whole new level; from the Peter Pan collar to the full gathered skirt to the bold purple and green plaid material.

I attempted to hide the garb from hell in my closet but my mother found it and promptly returned the plaid mishap to its place of honor for my first day of school. There was no way I was getting out of having to wear the "purple beast" so I attempted to disguise it with a cardigan sweater that I could button all the way up to that purple and green plaid Peter Pan collar. It didn't matter that we were having a heat wave in September; that sweater was staying on.

As the school day wore on, the heat became unbearable. Now I had a huge wet perspiration stain under each armpit so I couldn't take the sweater off. I was almost looking forward to someone sitting me in the water fountain; at least I would be wet all over to match my underarms.

I fully expected to be tormented by the eighth graders, but to my amazement I seemed to be skating free. I shared my joy with a friend in the band.

"Are you kidding? He answered. "No one is gonna mess with you! You're Chuck's cousin."

The rough and not to be messed with cousin who told me I was adopted years ago was now my protector. We *were* family.

## CHAPTER 4

*living in a fishbowl.....*

I had been taking piano lessons since I was seven. According to my teacher, I progressed well and demonstrated an aptitude for piano. After our move my parents were able to send me to Peabody Preparatory for lessons. I guess that was one of the advantages my mother told me about. I had been recommended there by my previous teacher.

Soon my Saturday mornings involved a trip to Peabody for a piano lesson followed by a one-hour theory class. I do appreciate the musical education I received there although I am confident I wasn't thrilled about it at the time. "Normal" kids were outside playing or watching Saturday morning cartoons while I traveled an hour away to take lessons then had to spend countless hours practicing.

There was one girl that lived across the road. We soon became good friends. We had met the first day my family moved in when her Mom brought over a cake to welcome us to the neighborhood. Her family was of Italian decent and her last name was a verbal stumbling block for someone raised in a dominantly German environment. I shortened it and lovingly named her "Cheni." She was beautiful with a flawless olive complexion and a womanly figure well beyond her years. I, on the other hand, was battling acne and built like a stick.

The first time I had dinner with her family it pretty much freaked me out. There was so much hugging and loud conversation. At first I thought they were yelling and angry with each other, but I soon realized they were just loving on each other, "Italian Style."

Dinner at home was very different. We ate in the formal dining room with a beautiful chandelier overhead promptly at 5:30 p.m. every evening. May God have mercy on anyone who showed up late. Our evening meal was a golden opportunity for my mother to grill me concerning the day's events. The only movement at our table was when I sneaked food off my plate and down to Rascal, my dog. Rascal always sat beside me when we ate, especially if we had liver.

Mostly dark haired with big brown eyes, Rascal was my best friend; my refuge. I could tell her anything and she would just listen to me. She even let me dress her up in baby doll clothes. This little beagle had style.

The older I got, the more my relationship with my mother deteriorated, but Rascal was always there to comfort me. I was coming into my teenage years and Mother was all about control. Our relationship was a train wreck. My Father described us as "two bulls in a china shop."

The relationship between my parents and my uncle was showing wear and tear. My uncle and I had become close over the years and instead of calling him Uncle Gilbert I lovingly called him Unk. He attempted to come to my rescue over the way she treated me; acting as a buffer between my mother and me. She would then bend my Dad's ear about it which would start up an "energetic discussion" between the two men.

I had no privacy. The rule was that I had to sleep with my bedroom door open, no exceptions. It could only be closed while I was changing. I was not allowed to offer any verbal disagreement with her decisions. All of my feelings were stuffed down inside. I knew not to talk back or she would deliver a slap across the mouth. I felt there was no pleasing her and no way to verbally defend myself, so I became an expert at puffing, sighing, and rolling my eyes. I hated being in the same room as her.

I cannot recall any hugging or kissing from my mother until it was time for me to go to school in the morning. Even though I was a teenager, I was required to kiss her at the front door before leaving for the bus stop. Not just on the cheek, but it had to be full on the lips. First off this was totally gross and second, everyone from the bus could see. I was so embarrassed. One morning I made a run for it, flying out the front door. I was halfway to the bus and beginning to feel confident in my escape when the yelling began.

"You better get back here right now and kiss me if you know what's good for you!" Now everyone on the bus was straining from their seats for a view out the windows to witness my drama. Back to the house I went to give my mother the kiss she demanded. I was totally humiliated.

Sometimes I went into my room simply to hide in the dark in my walk-in closet. It was the only place I could cry with no one to see or judge me. A place of retreat and peace.

One evening while I was visiting my friend Cheni, she called me over to her window. Our home was a rancher and hers was a two-story house on a slight hill. We were on the top floor and could see down on my home from there. She had a new pair of binoculars she was trying out.

"You're not going to believe this," she said.

I pressed the binoculars against my face and realized I could see straight into my house from there. The lights were on in my room. My mother was systematically going through all of my dresser drawers.

Sadly, I was not surprised. I felt violated and embarrassed. Like I said, there was no privacy.

In 1964 the Beach Boys had a hit entitled "In My Room."

*There's a world where I can go*

*And tell my secret to*

*In my room*

*In my room*


*In this world I lock out*

*All my worries and my fears*

*In my room*

*In my room*

*living in a fishbowl.....*

*Do my dreaming and my scheming lie awake and pray*
*Do my crying and my sighing laugh at yesterday*

*Now it's dark and I'm alone*
*But I won't be afraid*
*In my room*

I could relate strongly to this song and sang it often. However, I could change the words to in my closet, in my room. I used to day dream someone would come for me; that maybe there had been a mix-up in the hospital where I was born, wherever that was and my mom was looking for me. Perhaps I was a princess hidden away for safekeeping. I was haunted by an unknown past. Maybe something was wrong with me and that's why I was left behind, unwanted.

# CHAPTER 5

*"the look"*........

I knew better than to bring the subject of adoption up. That conversation would hail down bolts of ugly. My mother was a five foot two full-blooded German with dark hair and piercing eyes. When she had you in her cross hairs her forehead and thick brows would tighten. Oh yes, first came "the look," then great heaping mounds of guilt. "We chose you over twin boys. I don't understand what the problem is. Why do you need to know? We weren't given any information about the girl that had you."

I was told that my lineage was German and Irish, that my mother played the piano, and that she was pregnant with me when she was sixteen. Where did all of that information come from?

I had a good relationship with my Dad; but I didn't get to see him that much. He was a policeman for Baltimore County in Maryland and worked swing shift. For two weeks it was 3-11 p.m. He left for work before I got home from school and I was in bed when he got home. Then he worked 11 p.m. to 7 a.m. and he was in bed when I got home from school and getting up for work when I was going to bed. Finally, he worked 7 a.m. to 3 p.m. and I saw him when I came home. The shifts lasted two weeks each. Without Dad, my mother ruled the kingdom.

Dad had really wanted a son to name Joseph after his father. My mother wanted a girl, so a girl it was. They turned Jo into a girl's name; Joanne. Our daddy/daughter time was spent fishing, going to the theater to watch John Wayne movies, and my very short career playing on a girl's soft ball team. I hated soft ball. As I got older I introduced Daddy to shopping and that was fun. He let me pick out clothes that I liked as long as they passed the "sit test." I needed to find a chair in the store where I could sit down like a lady while wearing the dress. As long as all of my "lady parts" were adequately covered, he bought the dress.

By the time I was fourteen I'd come to the realization that my birth mother must have gone through a great deal to "give me up." I wondered if she ever got to see me or to hold me. Why didn't she keep me? Did she die during childbirth? I had so many questions. I made a point beginning on my fourteenth birthday to pray for her on every birthday. I continued every year after that. I felt closest to her on my birthday. If she was still alive, I believed that was the one time I could be fairly confident that she was thinking of me. I prayed that she had found happiness, was healthy, and had a good life.

*young love....*



## CHAPTER 6

*young love....*


I had a boyfriend and his name was Donald.  We met each other in fifth grade when he transferred into my elementary school.  He told me both of his parents were deceased and he lived with his grandparents.  I told him my special secret, that I was adopted.  That seemed to be our initial connection.

Over the years our friendship grew into romance.  Donald had brown hair and blue eyes and was over six foot.  The boys had finally grown taller than me in high school, and he was so handsome.  He asked me to "go steady" when we were in tenth grade and he gave me his class ring.

At first I only wore his ring in school until I could find the courage to tell my mother.  I wanted to avoid the drama.  Then, I had a brilliant plan.  It was cowardly but it was all I had.  I waited until we were sitting in the pew at Trinity Lutheran Church on Sunday morning and slipped it on my finger.  She looked down, grabbed my hand, and shot me "the look."  I knew that I would

27

hear about it later, but for one hour, I had peace. Sweet!

On January 30, 1968, I turned sixteen years old. When I came home from school that day I noticed nothing out of the ordinary until I hung my coat in the hall closet and headed for my room. The door was closed. That was odd. As I opened it, I saw that Daddy was standing in my room and there on my bed sat my mother.

"Surprise!" she yelled.

I looked around and my heart sank.

My parents had purchased an entire new black cherry Hinkle-Harris bedroom set equipped with a canopy bed for my birthday. Every piece of furniture previously occupying my room had been removed and replaced.

I never asked for this; never wanted this; but I knew I needed to be appreciative and show a happy face for the picture as the flash went off or all hell would break loose. Some may have considered me an ungrateful brat, but no one else had to live in that house.

I had once loved my antique furniture, especially the turn of the century hand crafted secretary that used to grace a corner in my room. The front cover folded down to provide a work place for writing and doing my homework. There were also secret compartments disguised as ornamental wood carvings where I could hide my diary and love letters from my boyfriend Donald. In one of the compartments I kept my fountain pen and ink supply. It was all gone. I learned that my secretary had been given to Grandmom so later I was able to go visit and retrieve my treasures from their hiding place.

Every drawer had been emptied from the old furniture and the contents rearranged where she wanted them in their new black cherry home. I no longer had a desk in my room and homework had to be done on the kitchen table in full view of my mother while she prepared dinner. I felt like an animal at the zoo, caged, no privacy, my every move supervised.

Unk had built an addition on the back of the house for a piano studio so that I could practice whenever I wanted. He had it decorated in Asian décor with a fishpond and a waterfall in the room. Two sides of the room had glass sliding doors. An artist came to the house and hand-painted beautiful landscape scenes on the glass. There was a bamboo bar running half the length of the room. There were high-backed bamboo barstools. I loved eating my lunch out there. It was so beautiful.

29

One evening my boyfriend came over and we sat on the barstools in the piano room, talking. While still seated, Donald leaned over and kissed me.

Immediately, one of the sliding doors jolted open. There was my mother. She'd been hiding outside, watching us through the glass.

"Joanne, get over here right now."

This was not going to be good.

As soon as I reached her, she slapped me across the face. "You slut," she shouted. "You're going to get pregnant just like your mother," she spat.

Her final verbal assault was delivered with cutting execution.

I could see the shock on Donald's face and I was mortified; disgraced by her outburst. God forgive me, but I hated this woman.

# CHAPTER 7

*College bound.....*

I graduated from Franklin Senior High School in 1970 and went on to study music education at Towson State. If you lived less than 35 miles away from the college you had to commute. Unfortunately, I lived close enough to commute which meant I would live at home with my mother. Unk gave me a car for my eighteenth birthday which enabled me to drive to Towson on my own. He treated me like a daughter, so generous, and I was very grateful for that.

Over the years Unk and I had become close. He took Rascal on car rides with him in the afternoons and even laid my sweet dog on his lap in the evening while he watched T.V. This is the same dog he had wanted to get rid of. In so many ways Unk had become a second father to me and I loved him very much.

I do believe Unk was as hardheaded as my mother and the two cousins often got into some intense arguments. His drinking added fuel to the fire. My mother dragged my father into the

31

middle of it and the ferocity of the "discussion" escalated. The writing was on the wall. This living situation would not last forever.

After living together for ten years, my parents, the dog and I moved out into a two-bedroom apartment. I was nineteen and Unk had offered me the option to stay behind with him. I was torn. He and I had a great relationship. He even offered for Grandmom to come over and live with us but she didn't want to leave her home. I totally understood, I didn't want to leave my home either. However, I felt guilty not going with my parents.

The close quarters of that apartment stirred the already difficult relationship between my mother and myself. Add to that the lifestyle change. We three went from a large home with a maid, a gardener, an in-ground pool, and lavish surroundings to a middle-income family, living in suburbia in an apartment complex. My piano was placed in the living room right beside the T.V. so there was no practicing in the evening after school. I needed to stay at college later in the evening to study and practice.

In October of 1971 I received a letter of invitation to join the Mu Phi Epsilon international music sorority. This was a pretty big deal. A young woman needed to excel in music with an outstanding GPA in order to be invited as a member. The cost was fifty dollars and you needed your parent's permission to join. They also sent my parents a separate letter explaining what an honor it was and the professional opportunities that would be afforded me as a member. The letter was written by hand and read as follows:

*10/19/71*

*Dear Mr. and Mrs. Wilson:*

*Your daughter, Joanne, has been asked to join Beta Epsilon Chapter of Mu Phi Epsilon international music sorority. She has earned her invitation to membership by her fine scholastic average, her musicianship, character and personality.*

*Membership in Mu Phi Epsilon is valuable during college years because of contacts provided in the professional world, friendships formed with others interested in the same art, and the opportunities to perform and develop leadership. In after-college years these same opportunities continue through affiliation with an alumnae chapter.*

*We will be happy to have Joanne as one of our members and know that membership will be an incentive, stimulation and enjoyment to her. We are confident she in turn can add to the strength of our chap-*

*My Secret: Joanne E. Sayre*

*ter as it fulfills the purposes and ideals of Mu Phi Epsilon.*

 *Sincerely,*

 *Cathy McGowan*

 *President*

I worked part-time at Hess Shoes in the local shopping center and was willing to pay the fifty dollars; however, my mother said that she didn't like my attitude and I was not allowed to join.

Neither of my parents had attended college and were not aware of the gravity of this opportunity. I attempted to plead my case. I explained that the connections I might make would last throughout my teaching career. The sorority wrote another letter to my parents requesting their consideration. Once again my mother refused.

# CHAPTER 8

*An act of war.....*

In November 1971 I started dating a young man that my parents disapproved of. His friend John and my friend Ginny were brother and sister. Chris had long hair, wore a headband, and had a peace sign painted on the trunk of his car. I do need to state that, in his defense, he was exceedingly intelligent and courted me with love poems and flowers. Their disapproval made the relationship even more attractive since I was entering into rebellion mode. We got engaged and planned on a June wedding.

For once, I had some control over my life, no matter how poorly executed. And, yes, that is referred to as "cutting off your nose to spite your face."

I believe if you suffocate any living being with total control, freedom arrives in a panic state. Without the experience of decision-making, how can anyone develop a constant by which to govern their decisions? When a baby learns to walk, success is generally the result of learning from the failure of previous attempts. Eventually, the child keeps trying and is rewarded with their newfound freedom; walking on their own.

By December I developed a bad case of tonsillitis and my parents took me to a doctor in a neighboring county who suggested removal of my tonsils. I was scheduled for a tonsillectomy the first week of January while Towson State was on break for their "Jan Term."

After surgery, I was unable to speak for at least two weeks. Three weeks after surgery I drove over to college to sing for my voice teacher. She started crying and told me that I would never sing again. Evidently, my vocal chords had been permanently damaged during the surgical procedure.

"Why didn't you come to me and use one of the doctors that we recommend to our vocal students?" she asked, her hand on my arm and her eyes earnest.

She didn't know my mother. That would have never happened.

I was devastated, walked off campus, and did not return. I felt as if life boxed me in at every turn. My life was imploding.

One week later, at the end of January, I turned twenty. My mother advised that because of my bad attitude, she had cancelled my June wedding. Yes, she threw down the gauntlet; backed me into a corner.

I'd had enough. My reaction? My fiancée and I went to the Towson Court House in Baltimore County and on March 3, 1972 were married. My parents chose not to attend. His father and five of our friends were there.

My new husband and I moved down to Arlington, Virginia, and I stayed out of contact with my parents for ten months. I heard from my cousins that my mother was taking bets that my marriage wouldn't last six months. I was determined to prove her wrong.

I, of course, realize in hindsight that marriage was my knee jerk reaction to events in my life I had no control over. There I was jumping out of the frying pan into the fire. However, no matter what the influences, I was responsible for my own actions.

## CHAPTER 9

*The search begins.......*

In 1973 when I was twenty one years old I began to search for my birth mother. I joined a group in the Northern Virginia area called Adoptees In Search (AIS.) This was a support group purposed to assist adoptees in navigating through the search process. They gave me suggestions on how to begin my search.

I contacted the Vital Records Department in Hanover, Pennsylvania to receive my original birth certificate since my mother had told me that that was where I was born. Surprise! There was no record of my birth in Hanover.

During a visit to my parents I confronted them with my new found information.

"Since I work for the government, the accuracy of my background check is vital. They're going to think I'm trying to hide something." Yes, I stretched that one a little.

Daddy said, "I don't know where you got Hanover from. You were born in Philadelphia."

My mother appeared agitated and tried to stick to her Hanover story until Daddy insisted that it was Philadelphia.

Thank you Daddy. I could tell by my father's face that he had no idea what the problem was. My mother clearly understood that my search had begun. This was her attempt to throw me off the trail.

I contacted the Department of Health and Vital Statistics in New Castle, Pennsylvania, requesting a copy of my birth certificate for Philadelphia. I received a letter back from the Assistant Director for Operations:

*We are in receipt of your request for a certified copy of your original birth record, before adoption.*

*Please be advised that the original record filed for your birth was a delayed birth registrations, filed at the time of the adoption. No original birth record was filed previously. Therefore, we are unable to furnish the pre-adoptive information requested.*

*We truly regret our inability to assist you in this matter. Enclosed is our refund check representing the fee submitted.*

This information was unsettling to say the least. There was no "original record filed for your birth." Who doesn't file an original birth certificate in this country? I believed it was a felony not to have filed one.

I took the letter to my next AIS meeting to seek additional help. No one could believe it. Their only suggestion was to look at my immediate family. Many times a baby is born out of wedlock to someone in the extended family and adopted by another member of that family. Perhaps I had distant relatives in Philly. We had a pretty small family.

Chris and I shared this information with our friends Ginny and John. They felt they needed to tell me something their mother told them. The word in the neighborhood was that my Aunt Elsie was my birth mother. What? The woman had seven children. How would that even be possible? I just stored the information away under backyard gossip. It seemed every turn I made I found a wall; no facts, just more questions.

It was now the summer of 1977 and I was pregnant with my first child and nausea was the word of the day. My commute on a Trailways bus to work didn't help either. My breakfast consisted of sipping on Coca Cola while snacking on Saltine Crackers.; the breakfast of champions, or of pregnant women that can't keep anything else down. This went on for almost five months.

I continued my commute from Manassas, Virginia to Washington, D.C. until I was two weeks overdue. My hospital was located in D.C. I would be a lot closer than if I was at home.

Our marriage was showing signs of wear and tear. I had hoped that Chris and my relationship would be stronger after the birth of our baby. I was wrong.

"Back in the day" the sex of the baby was not known until that final push. It didn't matter to me whether I had a boy or a girl. I just wanted my baby to be healthy. My beautiful son Shawn was born in the spring of '78. Since his full name was obviously Irish, the staff at Georgetown University Hospital drew shamrocks on his identification card in the basinet. I wanted to hold him all of the time and stare at him. He was actually a part of me. Amazing! I was no longer alone.

It was difficult to return to work after eight weeks and leave Shawn with his new caregiver, Mrs. Noonan. She was a wonderful babysitter, but she wasn't me. I couldn't wait to return home from work each day and hold him.

Caring for my son, working full-time, and commuting two hours each way to work in D.C. left little time for anything else. My search hit the back burner.

When Shawn was only a few weeks old his father and I travelled home to Maryland for a visit with friends and family to show off my beautiful baby. As we pulled up to my parent's, I noticed Pennsylvania plates on a vehicle parked in their driveway. I realized that my Aunt Elsie and Uncle Donald must be visiting as they had moved to Pennsylvania several years earlier. As I walked into the kitchen carrying my son, my aunt rushed over and scooped him up. She lovingly held him close to her and laid her cheek on his face.

My mother said, "Shawn, say hi to your Grandmom."

Awkward. There was a brief silence as the two sisters stared at each other. Then my mother said, "Well, you know, she's always treated you like one of her own."

Score! I thought surely this was evidence that all of the rumors were true. The neighborhood rumor mill proclaiming my Aunt Elsie as my birth mother. It all made perfect sense; the constant bickering between the two sisters, the intense jealousy of my mother towards her sister, and the fact that there was an age gap between her fourth and fifth child. I fit right in there. Perhaps I was too hasty in my earlier dismissal of this possibility.

My oldest cousin Martha Ann was ten years older than me so I went to her and asked if she remembered anything that could help me sort this out. She gave it a great deal of thought but she couldn't remember anything.

I knew I needed to file this encounter away in my ever increasing "info that goes nowhere" folder.

# CHAPTER 10

*And life goes on........*

When my son was a little over one year old his father and I separated. It was a difficult and unsettling time. We had been married almost eight years. I was now out on my own with my little man.

I signed over the house to my ex and rented a two bedroom condo just down the street. By the time I travelled home from work, picked Shawn up from the sitters, made dinner for the two of us, and bathed him, it was pretty much time for us to go to bed so that we could get up in the morning and do the whole thing over. I must have been worn down more than I realized because I developed double pneumonia. It soon became obvious that I needed help with my son. He needed to be my priority. So, I did what I swore I would never do...I moved back to Maryland and in with my parents for six months.

After three weeks, I was able to go back to work. It was still a four hour round trip to work. The relationship between my mother and I had not improved; however, I appreciated the help. Daddy and his grandson became very close and it was good for both of them.

After moving back home, I'd reconnected with some old friends from college. We'd all been music majors together. One of those friends was a guy named Michael whom I had dated while attending Towson. He'd never married and asked if we could enjoy dinner together one evening. One evening developed into several evenings and then many months. The relationship became serious. I was beginning to enjoy my life again.

Michael was a working musician. Whenever possible, I accompanied him to his gigs. I enjoyed music again.

The three of us attended Saint Patrick's Catholic Church in Baltimore, Maryland where his father was a deacon. Both Michael and his father played trombone. They planned for me to accompany them on the keyboard for an upcoming service.

Michael's family embraced Shawn and me into their family. They even invited us "down the ocean, Hon" (Ocean City, Maryland) on vacation. Michael had two nieces that were a few years older than Shawn. The girls loved "taking care" of Shawn and playing with him.

While dating Michael, Shawn and I continued living with my parents. One night around midnight, Daddy came into my room and woke me.

"Joanne, hon, are you awake? I need to speak with you."

Daddy stood motionless beside my bed. The light cast shadows across his furrowed brow. "There's been an accident," he said.

It was midnight and I had been in a sound sleep but now the saliva rose in my throat as I waited for him to finish.

"It's Michael."

I immediately sprang out of bed in a panic, grabbing at my clothes to get dressed and go to the hospital. Daddy put his hands up. "Michael's not in the hospital," he said. Daddy's face was "stone cold serious." "The accident was fatal. Michael is at the morgue."

At the morgue. At the morgue. Those words just kept repeating in my head.

I didn't know what to do. I was hysterical, totally overcome with grief. Daddy sat down in his rocker and I curled up in his lap. Michael was only thirty. How could I explain this to my two year old? We'd had such a great weekend; my birthday weekend.

I was angry with God. If God really loved me, how could he let this happen? I felt like I just couldn't take anymore LIFE.

Michael's parents involved me with the viewings, the funeral, and the burial. It was very kind of them, but I was emotionally drained. There was nothing left in me — the fight to stand again had abandoned me. Without my son I might have done something stupid.

## CHAPTER 11

*A new beginning….*

After several months, I began to search for a place for Shawn and myself. One nice thing about living in the area again was hanging out with some of my cousins, especially my youngest cousin Lois. She had married in the past year and they were expecting their first child. They were renovating an old farmhouse that they were renting. Lois kept trying to fix me up with her husband's best friend but I turned her down. One divorce and one funeral was not a great record for relationships.

It was the first weekend of May 1981 and my parents were going camping in their RV for the weekend and taking Shawn with them. I knew he would have a great time hanging with Pop-Pop and sleeping in the RV. This was really perfect timing because I was busy packing things up to move the following weekend into my own two bedroom apartment. This would be a fresh start for me and my son.

Lois had just given birth to their daughter Shannon. I hadn't seen her yet so I thought I would take a break from packing and drop a gift off to her. I called first to see if it was a good time to pop in. She told me to come over as her twin brother Jimmy was also there. We could all hang out for a while.

The farmhouse was barely visible from the main road. The only marker for the driveway was an old roadside shed. The driveway wasn't paved and proved bumpy in areas washed out by a hard rain. As my van crested the hill, their home was in plain view. Smoke rose from the chimney. A freshly plowed garden was to the left of the house and to the right fencing that restricted the neighbor's cattle. This looked like a Thomas Kincade painting; peaceful, warm, and inviting.

Their dog Sam began barking, announcing my arrival. Lois's husband Dan greeted me at the door and led me into the living room where everyone was gathered.

While we three were talking, Dan slipped into the next room and called his best friend to say, "She's here." About thirty minutes later there was a knock at the front door and in walked a fine looking man with the most beautiful blue eyes I had ever seen. Mercy. I hadn't expected this. We all sat around and talked for quite a while. Their friend J.R. excused himself to another room and came back to hand me a note. Good heavens, this man looked as good walking out of the room as he did walking in. I read the note after he left. On it was his phone number with the word "anytime." This was a quiet man; however, still waters run deep.

He and I began to spend all of our free time together. The three of us had so much fun together that summer. We took full advantage of the pool at my new apartment. We enjoyed bonfires at Lois and Dan's farm, roasting corn from the garden. I rode on the back of J.R.'s motorcycle a few times. Unfortunately my fear of the bike won. When he would lean into the curve, I leaned the other way. This proved counterproductive.

J.R. and I talked hours upon hours about our likes and dislikes, and what we would never put up with again in a relationship. We had both been married and wanted to avoid another disaster at all cost.

We met on May second and on September sixth we were married in front of that old farmhouse where we'd met. We had fourteen people in attendance with Lois and Dan standing for us. It was also their first anniversary. Even though it was only four months since we'd met, we knew — when it's right, it's right. He

*A new beginning....*

was a keeper.

Life was finally turning around for me; happiness after a very long dry spell. My new husband offered for me to stay home with my son; no more babysitters. I quit work and my two hour each way commute to settle in as a dinosaur; a stay-at-home Mom.

## CHAPTER 12

*Our growing family…..*

Four months after saying, "I do," I was — pregnant that is. We were elated.  Once again I was feasting on saltines and coke. Because I was an only child, I did not want my son to be alone. This was such a blessing.

J.R. and I sat down with Shawn to tell him that he was going to be a big brother.  We explained that we had to wait until the baby was born to know if it would be a brother or sister for him. He looked very excited but ran into the other room.  About two minutes later he returned.  He advised us that he was going to have a brother.

"Son, we have no way to know that yet," J.R. told him.

Four-year-old Shawn replied, "I just talked to God and he said it was a boy."

Who can argue with that?

Lois and Dan were pregnant with their second child.  Lois was suffering with nausea the same as me.  Nausea to the side, it was fun to go through a pregnancy with my cousin at the same time.

Our joint anniversary was on September sixth. The four of us decided to go to a dinner theater to celebrate. Lois and I were "great with child" by this time.

After dinner and before the show we girls decided to make a trip to the ladies room. Of course we went together because that's what women do. No one else was in this four-stall bathroom so we each went into our own stall at the same time. There was one complication. The stall door swung in. My stomach was so big I couldn't exit the stall. I called for Lois. She too was a prisoner. Now what? All we could do was laugh and wait to be rescued.

After about ten minutes another woman entered the rest-room. I asked her to please help us. I had to straddle the com-mode as she pushed open the door. She just smiled and said, "Oh you poor thing." I thanked her and then asked her to do the same for my cousin. We returned to our table laughing. The guys said, "Wow, what took you so long?" Boy did we have a story for them.

Our baby was due on October twelfth but just like his brother, he came three weeks late. It took three trips to the hospital three nights in a row before John was born. Our hospital trips began on Halloween night. After the second trip I told J.R. that our baby would have to be waving before another trip to the hospital. I was scheduled to be induced on the morning of the third. I definitely did not want that.

Labor pains began again the evening of November second. J.R. ran our son Shawn down to the neighbor and by 11:30 p.m. we were on the road again. I went through transition on I-83. We arrived at Sinai Hospital in Baltimore at 11:57 p.m. I couldn't get out of the car. Hospital staff needed to get me out and transport me directly to the labor room.

John was born naturally at 12:57 a.m. on November third. He weighed 10.9 pounds and was 22 and 7/8 inches long. Let me just say that sitting was a problem for a while.

After John turned three I found myself yearning for one more child. The doctor told me if I wanted to have another baby they would have to re-suspend my bladder. I would also be looking at the possibility of a thirteen pound baby. J.R. and I talked and decided against that prospect and began looking into adoption. After all, I would be able to relate first hand to our child's feelings and questions.

We took our F.A.C.E class on May 2, 1987. This acronym

stands for Families Adopting Children Everywhere.  Instead of an extensive wait within the United States, we decided to adopt from Korea.  In hindsight, our Korean adoption process took more time than it would have to adopt locally.

We filled out all, and I do mean ALL, of the papers required by Catholic Charities to begin the adoption process for our little girl.  We were placed in an adoption group with four other couples, had in home visits, and MANY hours/weeks of classes on adoption in general.  Additional time was spent focusing on Korean adoption.

By the spring of 1988 couples in our class began receiving their assignments.  That is when you are matched up with a child.  Generally, the family waits another three months before their baby comes home.  But, we waited, and waited, and waited some more.  Everyone else had received assignments.  Why was our process taking so long?  This was the longest pregnancy ever!

We later found out that Korea had assigned a little girl, but our social worker felt the baby needed further evaluation.  He turned down the child, so they didn't present us with a new assignment.  Korea assumed we had turned down the child, so they didn't present us with a new assignment.

All of the members of our adoption group went to the airport in support of new arrivals coming home to join their forever families. It was an emotional experience, yet so exciting to a see moms and dads holding their new children for the first time. Each time a group of children came home, paperwork for new assignments came with them. Our social worker was confident that our assignment would be on the August 27 flight. He looked through the eleven folders while we were at the airport. I watched his eyes read the heading on each one and waited for that moment when he discovered our name on an assignment. Nothing came. I felt totally heartbroken. He assured us that, "The situation would be rectified."

That Monday morning, in a staff meeting at Catholic Charities, they reassigned paperwork for one of the baby girls and offered her to us. I immediately called my husband at work. He came home and we took the boys out of school to drive down to Baltimore City to see pictures and receive her information.

As soon as we saw our daughter's picture we knew the meaning of love at first sight. We eagerly signed the paperwork to get things rolling. Again, more paperwork; a mountain of paperwork. It took weeks to process all of the documents. There was passport information, banking records, proof of health insurance, and background checks on us including notarized statements from people who "knew us when." The paperwork seemed endless.

Finally, everything was in order. We needed to wait for her flight assignment.

Enter the '88 Olympics. Evidently, a well-known American reporter had decided to do an article on Korea "selling" its children. As a result of his article, Korean officials were considering a complete shutdown of the foreign adoption program. We needed lots of prayer. We felt so frustrated! We just wanted to hold our beautiful daughter.

After one month of deliberation, Korea decided to continue with the adoption program and began scheduling children for flights to the United States. For the sake of sensationalistic "journalism" this man almost cost many children their forever homes.

On December 2 our eight-month old daughter arrived. Family members, friends from church, and families from our adoption group came to welcome Nikia home. There were two other babies on the same flight home to Baltimore, coming to meet their families. It is pretty easy to pick out new parents amid all of the well-wishers gathered in the receiving area at an airport. They are the ones pacing, nervously anticipating the delivery of their child.

As the doors opened, the gathering became still; watching and waiting for all other passengers to disembark. The escorts for the children remain on the plane awaiting the social workers to board with the appropriate paperwork and take the child. It is necessary for the receiving parents to stand in an assigned spot to keep confusion to a minimum.

I requested that the social worker hand our daughter to her daddy first, just as I had done at the birth of our son John.

The flight staff disembarked and stood off to the side so they could view the "deliveries." Here we go! The first baby arrived and was delivered into the arms of her new mom and dad. My hands shook and I began to tear up.

The second child emerged; not ours. We knew that the next time would be our daughter.

Our boys stood on either side of me as their Daddy walked forward towards the entryway. There she was! I could hardly see through all of my tears.

Nikia was placed in her Daddy's arms and he walked over to join us. She was beyond beautiful!

*Our growing family.....*

This felt so surreal. As pictures were taken by friends and family, I dressed her in a snow-suit for our trip home. Babies arrive with only one bottle and the clothes they are wearing so parents need to come prepared.

When she was finally home our little family was at last complete. Upon reflection, there was no difference between the birth of Nikia's brothers and her delivery home; minus the labor pain and stitches of course, because the emotions were the same. The overwhelming and unconditional love that a parent has for their child is identical.

I made sure to keep every piece of paperwork on Nikia's background, medical charts, biological parents and her adoption so that one day she could read all about herself, her heritage, and her birth family. I kept it all.

## CHAPTER 13

*Back to school....*

In 1992 I decided to go back to college part-time and carry around six to eight credits a semester. Shawn was in high school, John in middle school, and Nikia was in kindergarten. I could attend one night class while their Dad was home and the rest during the day while they were in school. One of my classes was an English course in which we were required to write a research paper on a subject we were passionate about. My paper was entitled, "Adoption — The Seal of Secrecy."

My opening statement was as follows:

*According to the North American Adoption Congress in New York City, more than 60,000 people are currently involved in the search process. Birth mothers are seeking children they gave up for adoption, and children are hunting for birth parents. The search effort has grown in intensity in the last twenty years from an individual effort to a national movement (Cronin 90.) The search is made more difficult because adoption records are sealed by the courts. However, the rising sentiment in our society concerning adoptee rights provides stirring argument for removing the "seal of secrecy."*

After discussing the different types of adoption, I continued with an explanation concerning birth registries.

*Many states have responded to the sealed record issues with registration provisions. There are two types of registries, the mutual-consent and search-and-consent. A mutual-consent registry allows both individuals to meet, as long as the adoptee has reached legal age. The search-and-consent provision notifies the birth parents when the adoptee has registered (Sloan 39.) At that time, the birth parents can refuse to release any information. The adoptee is then notified that the birth parents are aware of the request. Birth parents can register their consent at any time, but they cannot initiate the search for the adoptee (40.) Although this is a popular procedure because it provides an exception to confidentiality, it falls short of fulfilling the adoptee's needs by requiring both parties' consent to share information (44.)*

*The State of Maryland has instituted a mutual-consent registry. It enrolls adoptee and natural families. The staff compares information and matches them. The information is confirmed with the agency and court records before the registrants are contacted by a social* worker. The natural parents of an adoptee may register at any time, regardless of the age of the adoptee. However, the adoptee may not register until he or she is over 21. Also, the natural siblings of the adoptee may not register until they are over 21. Although the place of birth doesn't matter, the adoption proceedings must have taken place in Maryland (Maryland Department of Human Resources 2.) There is a one time fee of $25 at the time of registration. Counseling is not required; however, counselors are available upon request. It is important to keep in mind that this is a mutual-consent situation. Therefore, if the natural parents do not want to be found, he or she may file an affidavit refusing release of names and addresses (3.) Since the court records remain sealed and can only be opened by a judge, the registry provides a viable avenue as long as both sides file. There are several support groups in Maryland that will assist in a search. One group is Adoptee In Search located in Bethesda, Maryland, and the other is Adoptee-Birthparent Support Network in Washington, D.C.

In a court case dated March 13, 1992, the Circuit Court of Montgomery County, Maryland was petitioned by a 22-year-old adoptee to open her file and provide identifying information. The adoptee expressed a strong desire to learn the identity of her natural *parents because of general medical and psychological concerns. Because of the constraints of Maryland law, the court denied the petitioner's request. However, the court recognized the need for additional legislative action, and deemed it appropriate to review the history of the sealing of adoption records in Maryland.*

*Prior to June 1, 1947, adoption decrees and pleadings were not routinely placed under seal. It was after legislative enactments in 1945 and 1947 that sealing such records became the norm (Ex Parte 1.) As a result of those enactments, Maryland Rule D80(c) "carries forward that all pleadings and other records concerning proceedings for adoption must be sealed." Maryland's sealing requirement paralleled many states, which in the 1920's, began instituting amendments of adoption statutes to seal the records.*

I continued on for many pages in support of my cause. Obviously, my focus was on Maryland law and my support of opening records for the adoptees. My final two paragraphs were as follows:

*It is unclear exactly who society is trying to protect by keeping adoption files sealed. The law states that it is trying to protect the adopted child; however, searchers are no longer children. They are grown, mature adults. It should be the right of every individual to know his or her genealogy, ethnic roots, and medical history. These*

*are privileges that the rest of society enjoys and takes for granted.*
*Adult adoptees are not looking for a new set of parents. They are*
*merely looking for answers to questions about who they are. Why was*
*I given up for adoption? What is my ethnic background? A door was*
*cracked open on October 12, 1992 by the signing of SB 61 requiring*
*mandatory placement of medical information in the adoptee's file.*
*A step in the right direction has been taken by the courts for future*
*generations of searchers.*

*I have been haunted with the prospect of beginning my own search*
*for many years. I'm not looking for a personal relationship with my*
*birth family, but merely answers to my questions. The decision to*
*search is a very personal and difficult one. It's a little like opening*
*Pandora's Box. One never knows what may be found. The truth*
*may not be the fantasy I imagined for myself; however, the puzzle will*
*be solved and the unrest will have ended.*

After writing my paper I contacted the State of Maryland and
filled out all the paperwork for the birth registry; however, there
was no match. Every time I ended up with a "sorry no match" or
"sorry we can't find any record of you," I took some time off from
my search. It was emotionally draining. That being said, I had
no intention of giving up.

Years went by with no further information, just rumors and gossip. My relationship with my mother continued its downhill journey. I felt that I could do nothing right. Here I was a grown woman with three children and still starving for some sort of positive feedback from her.

Admittedly there were times, however short lived, when she would say or do something loving or tender. I would get pulled in; let my guard down, then maybe a day later or even two days later...BAM! She was back to the cutting, sarcastic verbiage that I had come to know. At least when she was back to "normal" I could be sure of my footing.

We needed new furniture for our living room. Anything would be a step up from bean bag chairs. I invited my mother to go along with me and five year old Nikia to shop. My mother told me that upon purchasing new furniture and an entertainment center, she would give me the German clock that I loved. This family heirloom had been in the family for one hundred years. It stood twelve inches high, ten inches wide, and five inches deep. The encasement for the carriage clock was solid marble. The face was an intricate mosaic of colorful stones. I loved it.

With the furniture selected, a delivery date was set. My mother graciously attended its arrival. She provided direction to the deliverymen as to where she felt the furniture should be placed.

I waited several weeks and reminded her that I was ready to receive the clock. She said, "When you learn how to keep your house clean, maybe I'll give it to you."

It must be difficult to go through life angry; always calculating, ready to strike. I am confident there must have been some kind of undiagnosed mental illness associated with my mother; such a sad way to live. She only succeeded in blocking relationships and pushing family away.

Daddy was becoming forgetful, much more than usual, repeating himself incessantly. He had retired from the Baltimore County Police force twenty-five years earlier. However, in his conversations, those memories became current.

In the fall of 2001 my mother was diagnosed with colon cancer and needed surgery and chemo. That meant taking her for treatments and watching Daddy while she was gone. He could no longer be left alone. When he was away from her his only focus was only to be reunited with her as soon as possible. After sixty years of marriage, his emphasis was always on her. She was his linchpin. He seemed lost and unable to function without her.

It was hard to watch Daddy drift away. I recalled when he was young and I would watch him do backflips off the diving board. Where had the years gone?

After several months, Mother was on the mend but Daddy was getting worse. Senility is a thief. It steals your memories, good and bad. Daddy no longer knew who I was and that hurt me to the core. By the first of December 2002 he had to be placed in a special care facility for dementia patients. He had become para-noid and violent.

Daddy was only there for three weeks when we received a call that he was found in his bed unresponsive. He was transported to the hospital by ambulance.

This was during Christmas break while Nikia was off school. She and I picked up my mother and headed over to the hospital. My mother had placed a code blue in his chart. This meant that the hospital needed to take every possible measure to keep him alive.

Daddy had been placed on a ventilator. Dr. English advised that this was painful for him and requested my mother to remove the code blue. She refused.

"All of his organs are shutting down," Doctor English said.

"God is calling him home and you are preventing him from going. Mrs. Wilson, what we are doing is causing him great pain. Please let him go peacefully."

Again, she refused.

I said, "Mother, do you really want Daddy to suffer in all this pain?"

She finally agreed to let him go.

Doctor English thanked me for my intervention and took my father off all life support. He advised that Daddy could hear us and we should speak to him. We all told him how much he was loved and I told him that it was okay to let go. We said our goodbyes.

Once in the hallway my mother looked up abruptly and said, "Okay, I'm ready to go now." The doctor looked startled. "Aren't you going to stay with him while he passes?" he asked.

"No, I'm done," my mother responded.

After sixty years of marriage, she was done. Her husband was drawing his final breath and she was done. She left him to die alone. It was just too difficult to deal with so she wasn't going to.

I took mother home. She called my father's brother, Bobby. Uncle Bobby and my cousin Connie drove to the hospital so that

Daddy would not be alone.

Nikia and I went home and waited for my husband to drive home from work. My plan was to leave Nikia with her Dad and return to the hospital. While I was preparing to leave the phone rang. It was my cousin Connie. Daddy had passed holding Uncle Bobby's hand.

## CHAPTER 14

*I once was blind but now......*

In February of 2006 I began getting nasty little headaches. The doctors said it was probably related to menopause and should eventually pass. Of course, when a woman is in her fifties, it seems like anything they can't explain is blamed on menopause. My endocrinologist suggested that I take an anti-depression medication that she said would help with menopausal symptoms. I was not depressed; however, these headaches needed to go and I was willing to try anything. I never knew when they would appear or what stimulated their occurrence.

It was now the first weekend of June and we had sixty-four people coming to the house on Sunday to celebrate our daughter Nikia's graduation from high school. I certainly did not need a migraine messing up the festivities.

I took my first anti-anxiety medication on Friday night after dinner. Within two hours I developed a horrible headache. Then the scariest part happened, the parameters of my peripheral vision began to constrict. My field of vision got smaller and smaller while the intensity of my headache grew. Although this was in no way humorous, it reminded me of an old cartoon where at the end the circle around Daffy Duck became smaller and smaller until he eventually was no longer visible and the screen went black.

By midnight I was blind. I took my headache meds and laid down with cold compresses. There would be no sleep that night. I was in absolute misery.

The next day I felt no relief and was still blind. The pain grew stronger and stronger. Anything in my stomach and bowels had long since left my body. My husband put me in his truck and we were off to the hospital. I held ice packs to my head and kept a bucket available for the ride, just in case.

If you have ever been in an emergency room you know that nothing is ever as fast as you want it to be. By the time I was moved into a room, I was writhing in pain.

A nurse hooked me up to an IV and gave me strong medication that still left a dull throbbing pain to deal with. They performed a scan of my brain to rule out any brain tumors. While lying on the table I remember thinking; *this could be the end of my life.*

71

Thoughts of my children and husband flooded my brain; the immense love I had for them and the regret I'd feel if I left them. I truly believed this was the end. I fully expected to meet Jesus.

The scan came back with no findings and since these professionals couldn't find anything wrong, they chalked it up to menopause. I was given pain meds and sent home.

At home I took the pain pills and promptly threw them up. Nothing was going to stay down.

As the effects of the IV wore off, I once again felt excruciating pain. I had delivered both of my boys naturally; but that pain didn't hold a candle to the kind of pain I was experiencing. The rest of that night was spent with cold compresses draped across my forehead and eyes. It felt like I had sand in my eyes; a constant irritant.

Early Sunday morning our boys and their spouses arrived to help with Nikia's high school graduation party. I was still blind, in terrible pain, and getting worse. My husband escorted me back to the hospital while our kids handled the party. There were sixty-four people at our house for a graduation celebration and we were at the hospital.

At the hospital I was once again hooked up to an IV. My best friend Donna had come along for support. This time while I waited to be seen, they put me in a "quiet room" that was dark. I couldn't handle any light. Evidently this room was used for violent patients, to keep them from disturbing everyone else.

It felt like an eternity before I was taken back to the exam area. This time the head of the emergency room returned to review my case. He was rather upset that I had been discharged the night before while still blind. He called an eye specialist who advised him to check my eye pressure. The pressure read sixty in both eyes. A normal register would have been in the high teens. I had suffered an extremely rare acute glaucoma attack in both eyes.

The specialist had my husband bring me to his office connected to the hospital, so he could have access to specialized equipment. I was still blind and in incredible pain. It was like trying to look through cotton with an extremely brilliant light shining into your eyes. As the doctor put drops in my eyes the pain melted away.

*Thank God!* I had just spent two days and nights in the worst pain of my life.

Two days later the specialist attempted to perform laser surgery on my eyes to relieve the pressure. It was extremely painful and unsuccessful. The type of glaucoma I have is angle closure so the purpose of the surgery was to create drains in my eyes for the fluid buildup to drain normally. This doctor was the best in the vicinity; however, he said my case was rare and he recommended that I go to Wilmer Eye Clinic at Johns Hopkins Hospital in Baltimore City.

Since my husband had already missed a lot of work, my best friend Donna volunteered to take me to Hopkins. She was not waiting for an appointment; she drove straight to the ER at Hopkins where we ended up spending the entire day.

I was still blind and rather weak from my adventures of the last week and needed to be in a wheelchair so I could easily be moved around. After several tests, the general intake doctors at Wilmer sent me downstairs to the Glaucoma Department.

Donna later told me there were five doctors in the room checking my eyes and reviewing my chart. Considering that Hopkins is a teaching hospital, the rarity of my condition posed an attractive learning experience.

Upon presentation to Wilmer my vision was 5/200 in the right eye and CF in the left. My corneas were extremely swollen. As stated on my intake papers, *"slit-lamp examination shows protec-*

*I once was blind but now......*

tive ptosis bilaterally. The cornea on the right shows a few punctate epithelial erosions, and on the left there is an inferior epithelial defect. The cornea also shows 3 plus corneal edema. The anterior chambers are shallow in both eyes. The lens shows 1 plus nucleoschlerotic cataracts bilaterally." That is medical talk for "these eyes are messed up."

I needed to be at Wilmer every other day so they could check my eye pressure. Once the cornea swelling subsided after the initial attack, the doctors attempted five more laser procedures (iridotomy) in each eye to provide pressure relief.

During this entire "adventure" I remained blind. Donna came over every morning to make me breakfast and check on me. She always kept me smiling. I believe she would've made a great stand-up comedian. We are quite the combination. She is a petite blonde of Scottish decent and I am a tall brunette of Irish/German decent. I introduced her to the doctors as "my best friend and entertainment center."

Evidently, news about my condition had gotten around to several church prayer groups. I had thousands of folks praying for me; such a comforting yet humbling experience. Then on Sunday afternoon, nine days after the initial attack, our pastor and all of the elders came to our house after church to anoint me with oil

75

and pray over me by laying hands on me.

Two days later I was back at Hopkins for one of my many check-ups.

The young intern checked my pressure and looked in my eyes. *"I need to get a different scope, something must be wrong with this one," he said. "This can't be."*

Off he went for a different piece of equipment to look inside of my eyes. After completing his exam, the young doctor excused himself, saying "I need to get the head of the department."

Now on this particular visit, our pastor's wife, who was a nurse, had travelled in with Donna and me. It was comforting to have Tricia along as our "medical interpreter."

The intern returned about five minutes later with several other doctors, everyone taking a turn to look in the scope. And then the head of the department came in.

Later Donna said it was like "the parting of the Red Sea" with the rest of the doctors clearing out of the way for "the boss."

He explained that my optic nerves appeared to be pink and healthy. "They should have been destroyed and grey after such an extended period of elevated pressure. I can't explain it," he said.

I knew what had happened and I quickly chimed in. "This is

the power of prayer," I told him.

Then the doctors told me they'd had little hope that I would ever see again. Evidently, there was only a ten percent chance that I would regain any of my vision. However, through God, all things are possible!

Six months later while walking the dog I felt another glaucoma attack coming on. I made two calls, one to my husband at work and one to my doctor at Hopkins. My husband rushed home at warp speed because my doctor said to get to the hospital immediately.

My right eye was not responding to the previous procedures and required an emergency trabeculectomy. As outlined in the Wilmer Eye Institute's glaucoma handout: *"This procedure lowers eye pressure by creating a leaking area for fluid from the eye in the eye wall. The procedure is performed with local anesthesia and intravenous sedation in the operating room on an outpatient basis."*

Now, here is my interpretation: they put you out, numb your eye, and then bring you back to just a little buzzed while they cut open your eyeball, create a new drain, and stitch your eyeball back up. I'm really glad I didn't know what they were doing while it was happening.

Two years later I developed scar tissue around the incision area, impeding the flow of fluids which regulate eye pressure and requiring the need to repeat the procedure. This time they also removed a cataract in that same eye. That procedure was more involved than most because during my initial glaucoma attack, my iris was permanently seared open and attached to my cornea. Fun. I'm turning into the bionic woman.

My eye condition is hereditary and since I had no information, medical or otherwise on my birth parents, there was no way to be forewarned of the impending doom. Before the attack my vision had been 20/20. The little "puff test" they do during a general eye exam does not expose angle closure glaucoma.

How does one say thank you to a best friend that puts her life on hold to care for you, feed you, pray for you, endlessly transport you back and forth to the hospital for extended exams, coordinate meals for your family; the list continues. Donna laughingly refers to herself as a domestic goddess. Translation: a housewife. She has a husband and three grown children; however, her twenty seven year old daughter is physically and mentally challenged, requiring a lot of extra special mom attention. God has truly blessed me with her friendship.

Recovery has been difficult at times; however, I am very fortunate to have the best doctors in the world available for my care, which will continue for the rest of my life. Most importantly, I never want to forget or take for granted the fact that God chose me for a miracle. John 9:25: *"One thing I do know. I was blind but now I see!"*

## CHAPTER 15

*To DNA or not to DNA......*

I knew the truth was out there; I just hadn't found the key to unlock the door. I needed to step back and review my information from a different angle. I was unable to definitively rule out the possibility that my Aunt Elsie could be my birth mother.

I realized that I needed to explore all leads until they proved out. All I had was a handful of maybes, could bes, and don't know for sures. What I needed was proof positive; a DNA match.

I enlisted the help of my friend Lynnda who works in a testing facility. I asked her what I needed to do or secure to have a test done. How accurate would it be? What is the possibility of error? Could she do the testing for me? I also inquired about testing with one of my cousins since that would be a lot easier to accomplish.

Lynnda advised that the testing would have to be with my aunt in order for there to be absolute accuracy. She suggested I secure her toothbrush or some of her hair. Okay...that was just too weird. I was ready to hear Plan B.

My other option was to obtain a sample of her saliva. It could be from an eating utensil. Lynnda said to just watch for an opportunity. As requested, I sent her my DNA sample so that she was prepared ahead of time when and if I provided her with my Aunt Elsie's sample.

Months upon months rolled by, and then an opportunity presented itself. I was invited to a baby shower for my cousin's daughter. I was pretty confident my aunt would attend since the expectant mom was her granddaughter.

I continued to wrestle with the idea of collecting a "sample." The day of the shower arrived. To complicate things I needed to pick up my mother and escort her to the shower. I was a nervous wreck. I put a small paper bag in my purse and we were on our way. Still, at that point, I wasn't sure that I could go through with it even if the opportunity presented itself. I am just not a sneaky person by nature and definitely not spy material. There was also the added pressure of my mother watching my every move.

At the shower I was greeted by all my cousins, and my aunt and uncle. She was there. My heart raced. Surely everyone there would see it trying to leap from my chest. I just didn't know if I could do this. However, it was the only way that I could know for sure.

The event site was beautifully decorated and as usual with our family, plenty of food was available. After all, that's the German way. Since this was held in a multi-purpose room at a condo, there were multiple tables set up for everyone to sit down and eat.

The food was served buffet style so that after you went through the line you went over to one of the many tables to sit down and eat. My mother sat with her sister at one of the tables. As I walked towards a table I heard my aunt say, "Joanne, why don't you sit here with us." Seriously? There I sat with my uncle, my aunt, and my mother.

Through all the small talk it was difficult for me to concentrate. All I could think about was that small paper bag in my purse. My aunt was in her late 80's and I really didn't see her that often. I didn't know how many more opportunities there would be for me to know the absolute truth of whether or not she was my birth mother. I realized this could be my last chance. I was desperate for the truth.

Soon it was time to clear off the tables so that we could all gather around the expectant Mom and watch her open her many gifts. Before I realized that I was speaking, I stood up and offered to throw out all of the used plates, napkins, and forks at the table. Everyone placed their utensils on their plates and handed them to me.

With my fingers on my left hand I separated the plates so that her utensils did not get "contaminated" by anyone else's. I cruised toward the trashcan in the back of the room and threw everything out while holding on to her fork. I slipped it into a clean napkin and then into my pocket, whirling around to see if anyone was watching, but everyone was busy.

I excused myself to the ladies room and transferred the napkin-covered fork from my pocket into the paper bag within the security of my purse. I was definitely not cut out for this line of work.

We enjoyed the rest of the shower and then I took my mother home. I could hardly wait to call my friend Lynnda and nearly dumped my mother out of the car.

Lynnda was surprised I'd actually gone through with it, and so was I. After I delivered the sample to Lynnda I had to wait. It would take a few weeks because Lynnda needed to ship it off to a facility in Philadelphia.

After what seemed to be forever, I received a call from my friend. She said that the test results had come back and shown there was absolutely...NO MATCH.

"Is it possible that I mixed up her fork with my uncle's?" I asked her in desperation.

"No," Lynnda said. "The DNA was definitely from a woman."

Bam! Another door slammed in my face.

At least now I knew the truth. She was not my birth mother. I needed to put my heart back up on the shelf and look at the result as necessary work on the process of elimination. All of the gossip I endured about my aunt was just that — gossip. All of the talk between the ladies in the neighborhood — gossip.

Time to rethink, shift my focus and look elsewhere.

## CHAPTER 16

*And the search goes on.......*

It was the fall of 2008 and I was back on my quest for truth; with renewed diligence, I was determined. I knew there could be times of discouragement, but I was going to see this through. Once again, I contacted Maryland's Human Services Agency and filled out all the paperwork. This time they assigned me a case-worker, Joanne Lindsay.

My initial contact with Joanne did not come until December. We talked about my case and the information she received. I provided her with copies of my adoption papers and my adoption birth certificate that had been filed eighteen months after my birth. We both enjoyed the fact that we shared the same name, Joanne, and that it was spelled the same.

She promised that she would open the case and let me know what she found. I received a letter from her dated February 18, 2009. It reads as follows:

## My Secret: Joanne E. Sayre

*Dear Ms. Sayre*

*I am writing to let you know that I just received some additional information regarding your closed adoption record. The document provided some very limited background information on your birth family, which I want to share with you. In this document, you were referred to as "Brenda, born 1/30/52." Brenda was born in a Philadelphia hospital and brought to Maryland by a social worker and placed in an approved foster home where she remained until she was placed in the Wilson adoptive home. In this document it went on to say:*

**"Brenda's mother came from a middle class family who has always been self-supporting. Her own mother died when she was only three and a half years old and her father remarried about four years later. Apparently all of the family have made reasonably good adjustments. When she was about sixteen, Brenda's mother left home and obtained work as a waitress in a small town. She seems to be a pleasant, attractive young woman who usually gets along well with people. Brenda's father and mother were not married. The putative father is a career Army man whose family had come from England to live in this country. He has been married before. Brenda's mother**

*And the search goes on.......*

**described him as an easy-going good hearted person who could**

**not accept responsibility. He had served in the Marines for**

**several years and in 1947 went into the permanent Army. At**

**the time, we were working with Brenda's mother, he had gone**

**to Korea."**

*I realize that this is very little information, but it is all that the record provided. Your adoption was finalized in Baltimore County, but not through the Department of Social Services, who would have had a more extensive record. A private agency had done the adoption. However, the record did state the birthmother's name, which is information that we did not yet know. By using this name, I will now attempt to locate your birthmother. I will keep in touch with you as I am able to make progress in this process. Please feel free to contact me if you have any questions or would like to discuss this new information.*

*Sincerely,*

*Joanne Lindsay, LGSW*

*Adoption Services, Baltimore County Department of Social Services*


This was definitely an OMG (oh my goodness) moment for me. All of those years I knew absolutely zip about my background and was beginning to think that I'd been hatched. For many years I'd been existing within an information abyss and now, here was one little paragraph that rocked my world. To me it was a "best seller."

I called Joanne and thanked her profusely. She said that she'd contacted the Maryland Children's Aide and Family Service to obtain this information and this was the entire amount of information they had on me in the court file. With this one paragraph Joanne had found the holy-grail, my birth mother's name. Now she had the necessary information needed to locate my mother. YES!

In the weeks that followed, Joanne ran my birth mother's stats through every search engine available — nothing. There was no record of her social security number, no marriage license, nothing. We were so close and yet I could feel that door slamming shut in my face again.

Well, I refused to give up. That one little paragraph had given me hope and I was not going to quit.

By law, Joanne could not give me my mother's name. She needed to find her first and if she was still alive, receive permission to divulge her name. This allows the birth mother some control over the matter.

Ms. Lindsay then proceeded to send out a generic letter to families in the area with the same last name. She was convinced that since I was adopted out of Baltimore County, Maryland, my birth family was from the area. We waited for a positive response; however, none came. Joanne had received a few phone calls but no one recognized my mother's name.

Next, Joanne visited a graveyard in Cecil County, Maryland where people with the same last name as my birth mother had been buried. I was happy that she was unable to find my mother there. This gave me hope she was still alive.

I felt so blessed to have someone so dedicated in my corner. I knew by law she could not give me my birth mother's last name, but I wanted to know if by chance it showed any ethnicity. Since I was raised in a German household I wanted to know if maybe they had tried to place me in a similar cultural environment as my birth mother knew. Joanne said that she could tell me that it was definitely a German last name. For me, this was another piece to the puzzle. I was part German and from "the paragraph" I concluded that I was part English. Admittedly, I was hoping for part Irish because that's what I had been told growing up.

As Joanne continued the search, she found that the hospital where I was born, Salvation Army Hospital in Philadelphia, Pennsylvania, no longer existed; also, all of the records before 1964 had been destroyed. Could this be any more difficult? Why would anyone destroy birth records? Wouldn't that be against the law?

Months passed and there was no more information available; nothing new had surfaced. Originally I had told Joanne that I would be satisfied with that small, little, life-changing paragraph. However, as time went on, that wasn't the case. The small amount of collected information toyed with my insatiable appetite for the absolute truth, driving me harder to find my mother.

ABC aired a new TV show entitled *Find My Family*. This was a show designed to help families reunite. It was developed by the same producer as *Extreme Makeover: Home Edition*.

As written by Robert Seidman on November 11, 2009, in the official press release:

*Each episode of the television series is a one-hour, self-contained show full of moving moments and tears of joy, when mothers, fathers, daughters and sons who lost touch for decades are reunited. With minimal information, the "Find My Family" team will begin the difficult and frustrating process of sifting through archives and track-*

*ing down records until they uncover the missing links. The in-person reunions will take place at the "Family Tree." A follow-up with each family will conclude each episode."*

The two hosts of the show, Lisa Joyner and Tim Green were both adoptees.

This was just what I needed, professional investigators to find my birth mother. I downloaded the application form and filled it out. Again, another extended form to fill out. Okay, so the whole country saw all of your business up on the screen. If this brought peace to my life, I was willing to forgo some privacy. This could be the answer, so I spent the several hours necessary to fill out the forms. Upon completion, I overnighted everything to ABC and waited...waited...and waited.

I never heard back from the show, I guess that's because it was cancelled almost as soon as it began. Door closed. Moving on.

Each January meant a phone call to Joanne Lindsay just to touch base and see if anything has surfaced. She'd then run the information through her search engines and find...nothing. I was always hopeful but January 2010, passed as did January 2011, with nothing new.

## CHAPTER 17

*For unto everything there is a season.....*

During the entire spring of 2011 my mother had not been feeling well. Her doctor had ordered a series of tests and I took her in to hear the results. After laying dormant for ten years, her colon cancer had returned and spread to her lungs and adrenal glands.

We went to see her oncologist and he ordered more tests. I took her to the many scans and blood workups that needed to be done. At her age of ninety-two the doctor did not recommend my mother receiving chemo treatments; however, at her insistence he prescribed a new pill that could help.

After I took her home I called the oncologist and asked how long she had to live if the cancer was not arrested. He advised that she had about six months. I then called her general practitioner and with his help, talked her into checking out some independent living facilities in our area for seniors.

*For unto everything there is a season.....*

She was adamant about not leaving her home; however, she was having problems with fainting and incontinence. I found the nicest facility in the area, one that her doctor had recommended and we took a tour. By the end of the tour I had talked her into giving them a deposit for an apartment. There were only two apartments available and in order for her to get the one she wanted she needed to sign the contract, give them a deposit, and move in three weeks. While the manager was filling out the paperwork for my mother to sign, my mother was nodding out. She was so weak she could not stay awake. I ended up signing her name to the contract and the deposit check.

I borrowed a wheelchair from the facility and took her out to my car. On the way back to her home I called the homecare nurse and she met me at the house to check her out. I wanted to make sure that she didn't need to go to the hospital.

It was obvious she could no longer live on her own and I knew the only way to get her out of her house was to offer an independent apartment. One building over was the assisted care facility. If she was already under contract for independent we were guaranteed a place in assisted living when the time came.

I needed to get her packed and moved by September first.

This was an immense undertaking considering that she and Daddy had lived in their home for forty years, threw out nothing, and loved going to yard sales. Three bedrooms, closets, and a basement filled with "stuff." I guess it's the depression era mentality; throw nothing out. You never know when you might need three deviled egg containers.

I did most of the packing and she directed what was to go. I believe her intent was to try and fit everything from the house into her new one bedroom apartment.

Moving day came and one of her friends came to help along with my best friend Donna, the "domestic goddess." My husband had moved all of the antiques and helped back at the house trying to clear out the cabinets, etc. I had hired movers for the furniture and many, many boxes. By the end of the day we were exhausted!

In the days to follow, my husband and I sat up several eight foot tables in my mother's house to stack all of the glassware, plates, serving dishes, etc. that were in cupboards. The task seemed endless.

Meanwhile, after moving into her new apartment, my mother was getting friends to take her over to her house and cart out more "stuff" to her new place. This woman was a force to be reckoned with.

It was quite an ordeal to get her moved in and to get the phone and cable hooked up. I would call her in her new place to check on her and she would answer, "Welcome to the morgue."

Finally, after one week, she started going down to social gatherings and meeting people. Now she liked it. After almost three weeks there, one of her friends called me and said that my mother wasn't answering her phone. I checked with the facility and found my mother hadn't been down for any meals that day. So, at 8:30 p.m., I drove to the facility. I called ahead so security would know that was coming. They sent a nurse to check on her and then called the ambulance. The ambulance was pulling in at the same time I arrived.

She was rushed to the hospital and remained there for several weeks. Tests revealed the cancer was spreading and that at most, she had only about two months to live.

I had promised my mother that she would not be put into a nursing home, so I secured a place for her in the assistant living building and contracted hospice care for her. That meant moving her things once again; returning most of her belongings back to the house.

She moved into a beautiful little apartment on the corner of the building with big windows so that she could watch the leaves turning colors and the deer grazing in the meadow at dusk.

I had hoped we could find peace together in the little bit of time she had left on earth, but I guess not. She continued to introduce me as her adopted daughter. There were no parting words of encouragement, no I'm proud of you, no nothing. It was to end as it always had been between us.

She was there only two weeks. The doctor had spoken with her and so she realized she was in her final days. Her pastor had visited and had given her Holy Communion. She told him that she was concerned about her silverware and what I was doing with her money in her checking account. He tried to explain that I was paying her bills. Those words fell on deaf ears.

There is a verse found in the Holy Bible that addresses the situation, Matthew 6:21, *"For where your treasure is, there your heart will be also."* It was obvious to me I was not her treasure.

Now, extremely weak, she needed to remain in a wheel chair. I realized how immensely difficult all of this must be for such a highly independent woman. It had become necessary for me to spoon feed her dinner and put the straw up to her lips in order for her to drink.

When I returned the next morning the plan was for me to distract her in the next room by playing the piano while they disassembled her bed and setup a hospital bed. However, she was so out of it when I got there that they just went ahead and placed her in the hospital bed. It was too difficult to move her around in her queen-sized bed without pulling on her which was painful for her. Hospice had been called in and I was advised that it would probably be about three days before she passed.

I visited often and read the Bible aloud when I sat with her. One of the verses I read was John 14:2: *"For in my Father's house there are many mansions, if that were not so, would I have told you that I am going there to prepare a place for you?"*

She knew I was there but chose not to communicate with me.

I took an extended break from teaching piano so I could be there most of the time. I needed to run out to the doctor and drug store to pick up her liquid morphine, additional adult diapers, pay her bills, do her banking, etc. I had power of attorney; however, she had not been declared mentally incompetent so it was very difficult managing her affairs.

She surprised everyone by holding on for eight more days. During that time she responded to her friends when they came to visit, but not to me. I went out for lunch with my daughter on her last day and when I returned I found her unresponsive and ran to get the nurse.

"Honey, she's gone," the nurse told me after checking her. "It probably happened within the last five minutes."

It was November 19, 2011.

My tears flooded my face. Even after driving home I found it was hard to breathe. I mourned her passing. Mostly, I mourned a life that she'd spent angry with endless lost opportunities to love and be loved.

Our children helped us clear her room at the assisted living facility and move things to Goodwill and back to her house. Since I was an only child, I was responsible for coordinating with the pastor, the funeral home, the move, and everything else involved with a parent's passing. I was so thankful for my husband, children and good friends and that I was able to lean on them.

We needed to clean out most of her drawers before we could move them. During this process, I found a letter she had written to me. She had started it back in 1968 and outlined all of the many ways in which I was a disappointment to her. She even made additions to the letter through the 90's. Lovely.

The funeral was now behind me. I knew I needed to heal. I had met my obligations, done all that was required of an only child, and could very honestly say that I was free; no more guilt. Indeed, *I was free,* and it was time to move on.

## CHAPTER 18

*Let's get serious.........*

After speaking with my friend Lynnda, the DNA expert who works with the Baltimore City Police Department, I received the recommendation of a highly respected private investigator. This gentleman was a retired police detective and presently working for R.L. Oatman and Associate, Inc., located in Baltimore, Maryland. I spoke to Rick on December 30, 2011 and sent him a copy of all the paperwork on my birth and adoption.

In the early part of January 2012, I sent a letter to Joanne Lindsay at Social Services giving my permission for Rick to discuss my case with her. The two of them began communicating on January 12. Rick tried every angle possible; however, without my birth mother's name he was at a dead end.

My birthday, January 30, has always been the most difficult time of the year for me. I do a lot of reflection. In this part of the country, January is at most times cold and blustery. It's a time for making large pots of soup and adding pleasure to the senses with the aroma of hot fresh bread finishing up in the bread-maker. But, mostly it was a reminder that my heart was unsettled. I needed answers. I needed the truth. Still, I felt so very thankful that my birth mother chose life for me.

On February 6, 2012, I sent Joanne another letter:

*Dear Joanne:*

*I enjoyed our conversation the other day. It is always a pleasure to speak with you.*

*I just want to say that I really appreciate your involvement once again in my case. I have come to realize that my search will not settle in my soul until I have exhausted all possibilities.*

A few weeks later I received an envelope from Rick the private investigator. I assumed it was my bill for his services. To my surprise, it was a note from him and a newspaper article. Rick said that he felt bad that he was unable to provide me with the results I desired; however, he had just recently read this article in the New York Times about Ancestry.com and the success that many adoptees had found in their search. I contacted him to express my thanks for his thoughtfulness and immediately got to work contacting Ancestry.com.

Once again I filled out more paperwork, but this time online. I was informed that there was a backup for the DNA kits and my name had been placed on the waiting list. Waiting? I should be used to that by now...but no.

One month went by with no word. Two months came and I received an email that they were still processing all of the requests. After almost five months of waiting it was the end of the summer and my "waiting patience" was gone, so I started calling. One young man that I spoke with said it shouldn't be much longer.

Another month went by and I called again. This time I spoke to a young woman who advised there was no record of my contacting Ancestry.com and I was not on "the list."

I was not a happy camper. She and I spoke for some time as I told her my story. The young woman said she was sorry for the delay with my DNA kit and promised she would personally see that one went out that day. I gave her my credit card information and joined Ancestry. Five days later the kit arrived. Hallelujah!

The test kit involved a sterile container that one needed to spit into for five minutes until the contents reached a specified level. For me, that was a whole new kind of gross.

Now it was late September 2012 and I received notification

from Ancestry with my DNA results. There were matches; several distant cousins and one second to fourth level cousin with a 99% match. I couldn't believe it. There was someone out there that I was actually related to.

Her name was Pat and she lived in Michigan. I contacted my new found relative immediately and told her my story. She was intrigued and committed to helping me search. I was elated to finally have something positive going on with my search.

Pat gave me permission to have full access to her page and information. Because I had nothing to go on, we didn't know if she was related through my birth mother or birth father. My DNA results showed that I was 17% southern European decent. This takes in Spain, Portugal, and Italy. Pat's maiden name was Garcia and her ancestors on her father's side had emigrated from Spain, so this looked like a strong possibility.

I spent hours researching her records and came across pictures of her aunts and her father when they were young. There was a strong resemblance to me with the dark eyes and dark hair.

My daughter Nikia was helping me with the computer research as I am after all "computer challenged." I told Nikia that Pat was from Michigan and since I knew that I was born in Philadelphia and adopted out of Baltimore County, the possibility of a connection was slim. Three connections had to be present: Baltimore, 1952 (the year I was born) and a young unmarried woman. Pat's father's family came from Baltimore and her one aunt had died at 16 in 1952. Had I found her? Was it really going to be that easy after all of this time?

Pat's one uncle was still living in Baltimore and she told me she would call and ask him, delicately of course, if his older sister had possibly died in childbirth or shortly thereafter. My mother (adopted) had told me my birth mother had me when she was sixteen so I thought this might be the one.

Then, Pat called and advised me that sadly, this young woman had drowned in 1952 while swimming in a quarry. Her uncle also said his sister had never been pregnant. Although I had not discovered the identity of my birth mother, I had found Pat through my DNA match and that connection was a source of great joy.

## CHAPTER 19

*Never give up.......*

On January 28, 2013, I called my social worker Joanne and requested that she once again contact the agency that handled my adoption. I wanted to see if they could find any additional information. Several years ago that agency had advised they were unable to locate anything further concerning my file, but I thought a fresh set of eyes might uncover some hidden treasure.

Joanne said that she knew someone there and would contact that individual for help. She told me to call back in a week.

On February 4, I called and left a message; no answer.

On February 11, I called and left a message; no answer.

On February 18, I called and left a message; no answer.

On Sunday, February 17, our pastor had encouraged us to be in the Word (read the Bible) longer each day. He also gave us Bible verses to support his sermon that we could look up and study during the week.

While I was reading in Matthew chapter 7 about Christ's

words on judging others I continued to read through to verses 7-9: *"Ask and it will be given to you; seek and you will find; knock and the door will be opened to you. For everyone who asks receives; the one who seeks finds; and to the one who knocks, the door will be opened."*

I closed my bible and began to pray out loud in a voice trembling with anticipation, thunderous in volume and cracking from the exhaustion of the journey. "God I am BEGGING you, this side of heaven, please let me see my mother! Lord, I am yours!"

Two days later, on February 19, Joanne Lindsay called me back to say they were working on something and should have some information for me very soon.

Joanne called again on February 21, and said that they had found my birth mother's last name in a search. A man with the same last name had died in 2003. When they pulled up his obituary, they found that he was survived by several family members including a sister; her first name, middle initial matching the man's last name (maiden name) and her married name was provided. With that information they were able to secure a current address for her.

Joanne cautioned me not to get too hopeful as it could be

someone with the same name. A general inquiry letter went out

from Social Services stating that someone had contacted them

and thought that he or she may be related and please contact

Joanne Lindsay at the county office.

Since the letter went out on Thursday, I figured this person

should receive it by Saturday or at the latest on Monday and

hopefully immediately call Social Services. Patience is not my

strong suit.

On Monday, February 25, I received a call from Joanne as I

was driving to Target to pick up a prescription. I only had a short

window of time between piano students to complete my task.

Joanne asked what I was doing and when she found out I was

driving she asked me to pull over. I jokingly told her it was okay,

she could just give me the bad news now. She insisted I pull over

and park my vehicle.

I have Bluetooth in my RAV and she held on until I pulled

into the Kohl's parking lot and put my vehicle in park.

"We found her!" Her words resounded in my vehicle. I

couldn't believe my ears. They'd found her? Tears flooded down

my face. After forty years of dead ends, of "Sorry we can't find

anything, sorry there are no records on you," a constant parade of negativity... and now, here it was.

*She is real and they found her!*

Joanne told me that my birth mother had called to see what the letter was about. Joanne then asked her if she knew anyone that was born in Philadelphia, Pennsylvania on January 30, 1952. The woman, my mother, began to cry and said, "You are talking about my daughter."

Joanne had asked her if she would receive a letter from me, but my birth mother said that she wasn't sure. Joanne told me she thought my birth mother was trying to process the shock of being found. "She said that she had never told anyone about the birth except her husband who was deceased and she didn't know what she was going to do," Joanne shared.

Joanne suggested that she take a few days to think it over and she asked permission to call her back in about three days for her answer.

After I hung up I sat in the silence of my RAV and wept. I was stunned. After forty years of searching I had found her. I had fully expected Joanne to tell me it wasn't her. I had become used to bad news and dead ends. This was an entirely new sensation.

I was an emotional mess that evening. I blathered this information to my husband and our children. We hugged and I cried. Then it was back to more waiting.

What if, after all this time, she decided to reject me? What if there was a reason she'd stayed hidden for so long? What if this was not God's plan?

*No!* I hadn't come this far to allow fear to reign supreme. It's okay to be afraid, but one cannot allow the fear of the unknown to cripple you from moving towards your goal. Sometimes, you need to walk forward in fear.

The next morning, February 26, 2013, I received a phone call from Joanne advising that my birth mother had called her first thing that morning. Yes, she would accept a letter from me and would return a letter to me. She had decided to tell her family and had learned from her daughter that someone in the family had told her about my existence years ago. She had been waiting all those years for her mother to want to share that information with her.

Now it was time for me to write my letter. My first contact with my birth mother, the woman I had been tracking down for forty years. I had written this letter in my head a thousand times but now that the time had actually come I wasn't sure what to say. I didn't want to ask too many questions and scare her off, but then again this may be my only chance to communicate with her.

I typed out my initial letter and also hand wrote it out and mailed it to Joanne Lindsay to forward on. At this point we could not know the names or addresses of each other as the law determines that Joanne will act as intermediary.

A few days later I received a phone call from Joanne. "Is that it?" she asked. "Forty years of searching and that's all you want to know?"

I explained, "I don't want to overwhelm her or scare her off."

Joanne advised that I rewrite the letter and ask the questions on my heart.

After I hung up the phone anxiety overtook me. I'd wasted precious time with the first letter. *Why hadn't I written it right the first time?*

It was late at night when I sat down to write the new letter. It had just begun to snow. As the snow lay on the ground I realized that God had provided an atmosphere for peace and calm. I forgot about the gravity of the task and the words flowed from my heart to my hands.

*Never give up.......*

*I am flooded with a sea of emotions as I write this letter. I have searched for you for almost forty years. I want to say thank you for my life! Every birthday since I was fourteen, I prayed that you were well, that you were happy, and that you had found peace.*

*I am very blessed; a wonderful husband, three great children (35, 30, & 25) and three beautiful grandchildren. The oldest two are boys and are married. Our daughter is the baby of the family. She is adopted and was born in Korea.*

*I am a private piano teacher. I studied piano at Peabody Prep until I graduated from high school and then went to Towson State as a music major. I am 5'8", dark brown eyes and black hair. Admittedly I have needed to "help" it stay black since I hit fifty.*

*This is a letter that I have written in my head a thousand times; however, now I am having trouble finding the right words to express myself. I want to know who I am. Do I look like anyone in your family? I want to know about you. I would love to hear about my birth, my ethnic background, if I have any brothers or sisters, and if there are medical issues in my lineage that I should be concerned about. I have so many questions, but I don't want to overwhelm you.*

*When Joanne Lindsay called to tell me that you contacted her and were indeed my mother, I was speechless; then came the tears. I must confess, that in time, I would love to meet you.*

*Thank you for receiving my letter,*

*Joanne*

This time I emailed my letter to Joanne Lindsay for her input and she responded, "perfect." I hand wrote the letter out in cursive for my birth mother and included a copy of the typed letter for Joanne. Hand written letters seem so much more personal and I wanted her to know how special this moment was for me.

Around here a few inches of snow on the ground causes panic to grip the area. Every public school closes, and people with four wheel-drive vehicles shift into survivor mode and run out for toilet paper and milk; I got in my RAV 4, which I affectionately call "Ruby," and off I went to the post office to overnight my letters.

The next day, Joanne called to advise that she had received my letter and had in turn mailed it out to my birth mother. Now we needed to wait for her response. Having spent so much time waiting, one would think that I would be a paragon of patience. Unfortunately, my "waiting skills" leave much to be desired.

A week went by with no activity. I knew Joanne was out of the office for a few days but I called and left a message for her to call me when she returned.

Upon her return to work, Joanne discovered that my birth mother had called and left a message requesting Joanne to call her. She called to tell me this.

*Oh no, I thought, maybe she changed her mind, maybe my letter was too much.*

At this point, it really didn't take much for me to drop into panic mode considering all of the emotions surrounding this connection.

But Joanne had called and spoke with my birth mother. Evidently my birth mother was nervous and didn't know what to say or how to respond to me. She was afraid I hated her and she wanted Joanne's advice.

*Hated her? That thought had never even crossed my mind.*

Joanne told her to simply speak from her heart and if she needed to, have someone help her.

And so there was more waiting.

Finally on Tuesday morning, March 26, I received a phone call from Joanne advising that she had The Letter. Instead of putting it in the mail to me she asked if I would like to meet her at a coffee shop in Owings Mills to sit and talk. She would personally hand me the letter.

My answer didn't take much thought. YES!

Since we had never personally met in the five years we had been working together on my case, it would be great to finally converse with each other face to face. I described to Joanne what "Ruby" looked like so she could find me in the parking lot. I was so excited that I arrived at least twenty minutes early. I felt like a kid on Christmas morning, ready to dive into that beautifully wrapped gift nestled under the tree. The anticipation was overwhelming.

Joanne arrived and after we greeted each other with a hug we went into the little coffee shop, we ordered our coffee and secured the only remaining table in the place. The tables were rather close, reducing any possibility for privacy. Joanne asked if I would rather go somewhere more secluded. At this point I really didn't care who was there or how close they were. I desperately wanted to read that letter.

We sat down and after some polite chit-chat Joanne handed me the letter. My hands were shaking as I gingerly opened the flap.

*"Hello Sweetheart."*

114

*Never give up.......*

That's as far as I got when the tears started running down my face. I looked up at Joanne.

"I know, that was my reaction also," she said softly.

I needed to take a moment before reading the next line.

*"I want you to know I have always loved you and held you in my heart."*

It became increasingly difficult to read amid my tears. I had never experienced such a love language between a mother and child. The letter was very short but went on for a few more lines. She signed it, *"I would love to meet you. With All My Love."*

At the bottom of the letter was a different handwriting. It said, *"I want to meet you too. I'm your sister Barbara."*

My sister? I have a sister? I was speechless, awestruck. My mind scrambled to make sense of all that was unfolding.

This letter answered none of the questions I had written out in my letter, but had said everything that I had ever wanted to hear. She had written a masterpiece. Joanne said she had never seen such a loving letter from a birth mother.

Although my voice was still trembling, I held tight to my letter and I asked Joanne to set up the meeting.

I'm ready; no more time spent wondering. I can't wait to follow this through.

I told my cousin Lois about my discovery right before Easter and swore her to secrecy until I knew for sure that we were going to meet. She and I have always been close and I didn't want this whole process to leak out without her hearing it from me personally.

She was able to share with her siblings on Easter when they all got together. By then I had received my birth mother's letter. I was concerned that they not feel hurt that my desire was so strong to find her. I was so relieved that everyone was excited for me.

One week after our meeting at the coffee shop Joanne called to say that "The Meeting" had been set up for April 17, at 11 a.m. at the Social Services building in Towson, Maryland.

*It's so hard to believe that this is actually going to happen,* I thought after I hung up the phone. I'm meeting my birth mother and my sister.

## CHAPTER 20

*The meeting is on.......*

April 17, 2013 came, the day of the meeting. I tossed and
turned in bed until 2:45 a.m. and then I got up to take half of a
Xanex that my doctor had given me to help me sleep.

By 4:15 a.m. with no sign of slumber, I realized my efforts
were futile and I might as well get up. I made a pot of coffee and
took my vitamins. I brought my coffee with me into the comput-
er/office room and I was followed by the dog and cat. They, of
course, had no problem going off to sleep.

*At 11 a.m. this morning I will be at the Social Service building
in Towson meeting my birth mother and sister for the first time. No
wonder I can't sleep!* I chastised myself. The anticipation was
all-consuming.

I had prepared a four by six photo album for her to keep. It
contained twenty pictures of everything from my growing up, to
pictures of our children, the boys — each with their wives and
children and our daughter with her boyfriend. I wanted her to
be able to take it with her so she didn't feel rushed at our meet-

ing. And I'd gone to my favorite florist, The Cutting Garden, to purchase a beautiful bouquet of colorful flowers.

I had waited a lifetime for this moment and it finally arrived. A cacophony of negativity crept into my thoughts. *What if she doesn't like me? What if she is disappointed in me? Oh please God, don't let her be disappointed.*

I have a sister!!! I still hadn't gotten my head wrapped around that yet. I was raised an only child. This was all foreign to me and I couldn't seem to stay focused. It felt like watching our dog chase a ball and then at mid-run go in a totally different direction because a squirrel runs across the yard.

Finally it was 9:45 a.m. and time to leave. Admittedly, I was excited, anxious, nervous, all of the above and all at the same time. My husband volunteered to take off of work to escort me to the meeting. I really needed him with me as this was a BIG day.

I was as ready as I would ever be. I was prayed up, coffee in hand, with flowers for my birth mother, and the photo album I'd made for her. God could not have provided a more beautiful sunny day. Even the traffic was minimal, "smooth sailing" all the way to Towson.

*The meeting is on.......*

We arrived at the Social Services building a half hour early. I called Joanne and she said to wait fifteen minutes, then come to the front door. My poor husband! I was stressing and had nothing to do for what felt like an eternity. Every two minutes I checked the time. I smiled, reminded of our kids when they were little and on a long car ride, "Are we there yet? How about now? How much longer?"

Finally, it was time to go in. My husband prayed with me before I left our vehicle. I entered the building, signed in at the guard's desk, and then waited for him to call Joanne down to meet me. We took the elevator up to her floor and upon exiting she led me through a maze of desks and partitions to a single "family" room. This area was designated for children in foster care to visit with their parents, prospective adoptive parents, counseling, etc. Inside the room was a table, a sofa, a few chairs, a coffee table, and a play area for small children with a variety of toys.

Joanne wanted to speak with me one more time before I met my mother and my sister to make sure that I understood these meetings were not always daffodils and fairy dust. She advised me, saying some mothers walk in and shake their child's hand

119

with a "nice to meet you attitude" and then walk out the door with a parting, "have a good life."

I really had no preconceived expectations of what this meeting will be like. Even though I was hopeful, I tried to be realistic. I just needed, with my own eyes, to see her face. I had waited all these years and now it had come down to this day, this time, this moment of truth. Yes, I hoped that she'd like me and would be comfortable having lunch to talk in a more private, less controlled and sterilized environment, but I knew she may just say "nice to meet you" and "have a good life."

Joanne's parting words were, "Don't expect an Oprah moment." She stood and turned toward the door and I asked for one last favor. "Please call me on my cell before you bring her into the room." I needed one last moment to prepare for her entrance.

When the phone rang I jumped.

This was it, they were headed to the family room. I prayed for strength and acceptance of whatever happened.

*What if she was short, with a walker, fragile, no teeth...oh my... sorry God, how petty of me. I am no better than anyone else. What if SHE doesn't like ME? I have come all this way and must have faith that the Lord is with me.*

I heard voices outside of the door and then the doorknob turned and there she was.

I swallowed and was unable to speak. My mother was beautiful; her silver hair done in a cute little pixie spike, nails polished in bold pink, gold hoop earrings, and she was walking straight for me. I couldn't believe it. She was taller than me! I couldn't see anything else, just her face. She walked right towards me and embraced me in an endless mother hug. *So this is how it feels,* I thought. Then my mother called me sweetheart. She said, "I love you. I have always loved you," and then she kissed me.

It was very hard to see through all of my tears but there was my sister too, crying, with her arms out to hug me also.

*I have a sister! I have a sister!! And she is beautiful, warm, and loving just like my mother.*

We finally sat down together on the sofa; one on each side. They made a "me" sandwich.

Once seated, I glanced over at my social worker Joanne and tears were running down her face. We talked for over an hour, sharing pictures, holding hands and occasionally crying together. It felt as if I had always known these two beautiful women and that we had only been separated for a while and once again re-united. It was such a strange sensation, very surreal.

The time flew by. I gave my birth mother the photo album and the flowers and she was so appreciative. My sister Barb asked Joanne how much longer we could have the room. Joanne said she was sorry, but only five minutes more as someone else had secured it for the following hour.

Mom looked at me, her face soft and full of love and asked, "Honey, would you like to get a cup of coffee somewhere?"

That was all I needed to hear. Message received. That was the cue that she and Barb wanted to continue our time together.

I told them my husband was waiting in the parking lot and would love to take us to lunch. They were excited at the prospect and so we prepared to leave.

Joanne led us out of the building, back through the maze, to the parking lot where my husband waited. I had previously said I would like to take them to lunch if things went well, so he was prepared. J.R. knew right where they had parked their car. He said, "I was sitting in the truck when they'd gotten out of their vehicle. I knew it was them right away because you look just like your Mom."

We wanted to go somewhere that we could talk fairly private-
ly so they followed us down the road to TGI Fridays at Towson
Town Center for lunch. As we drove my mind slipped back to
the conversation with Joanne in the family room when she'd said,
"Don't expect an Oprah moment." Actually, I'd received something better than that, I received a God moment! AMAZING!

The four of us sat at the table and ordered lunch. We three ladies just kept talking, and talking, and then more talking. I could
hardly believe I was sitting across from and looking at my mother
and sister. Our lives would forever be changed; every relationship
would be altered.

At one point, my mother said, "You know, I always knew one
day you would find me. I figured you would show up at my door
and say you thought I was your mother. I decided I would ask to
see your birth mark."

I laughed and told her that I'd needed to have it removed
when I was twenty but I would be happy to show her the scar.

My sister Barb laughed and said, "Mom, seriously, just look at
her face. She looks just like you."

They showed me pictures of my other sister Patty, who had
passed away seventeen years prior. She left behind two handsome

teenage boys and a beautiful little three-year-old girl. I regret never getting to meet her; however, I would have the joy of meeting her children.

Time flew by and before we realized it, it was 3 p.m. and rush hour would be upon us. We all exchanged phone numbers, addresses, and most importantly, our full names.

As we stood and prepared to leave, my mother took my arm and said, "When I wrote you that letter, I didn't know how to sign it. I didn't want to be presumptuous. I gave birth to you but it wasn't me who walked the floor with you when you were a baby. It wasn't me who raised you."

My head whirled as I heard her words. Then I asked her, "What would YOU like me to call you?"

She smiled and said, "Mom."

"Okay then, it's Mom."

We walked to our vehicles to say goodbye with promises of getting together soon and talking on the phone. There were more hugs and more tears. It had been a completely perfect day.

When we got home I called each of our children to share the day's events with them. Each had been waiting and wondering and hoping for my sake everything had gone well. Calls were